A CHRISTIAN PERSPECTIVE ON
CREATION VS. EVOLUTION

MICHAEL L. McCOY

CPH.
SAINT LOUIS

Edited by Rodney Rathmann

CONTENTS

PREFACE

ABOUT THE CHRISTIAN PERSPECTIVE SERIES

How often haven't we been confronted with an issue that challenges us? It nags at our patience, frustrating us in our desire to honor God in the way we handle, manage, and react to the issue in our daily lives. We struggle, unable to find the right approach or perspective. Some issues may even cause us to question God and His power and presence in our lives. At times we may feel helpless and weak in the way we react to an issue—baby Christians wondering if we will ever grow up. Feeling unworthy and ill-equipped to be the witnesses of Jesus in an unreceptive or apathetic world, we may echo the sentiments of Agur of old, who marveled at the greatness of God in comparison with his own inadequacies. He said,

> "I am the most ignorant of men; I do not have a man's understanding. I have not learned wisdom, nor have I knowledge of the Holy One. Who has gone up to heaven and come down? Who has gathered up the wind in the hollow of his hands? Who has wrapped up the waters in his cloak? Who has established all the ends of the earth? What is his name, and the name of his son? Tell me if you know!" Proverbs 30:2–4

Fortunately, God didn't leave us alone to struggle with those things that challenge us and cause us to pause when we don't know what to think or how to respond. With a love for us that reaches back before the beginning of time and connects us with a crude wooden cross that stood in Palestine some 2,000 years ago, God cares about our everyday concerns. He has given us the direction, counsel, and forgiveness of His holy Word to help us live lives in joyful response to all that He has done for us through Jesus, His Son and our Savior.

Each title in the Christian Perspective series has been designed to provide the insights and reflections of an author who has personally confronted an issue that touches us and challenges our lives of faith in one way or another. He or she has sought the counsel and application of God's holy Word to this topic and has put his or her thoughts and conclusions in writing to give others confronted with the same issue a "jump start" in their thinking.

The Christian Perspective series has been designed in the book-study format, organized in chapters and suitable for either individual use or group study. Following the reading of each chapter, questions have been provided to further stimulate your thinking and to serve as discussion starters if the book-study is being used in a small-group setting. May God bless you as you explore the topic of this course.

SUGGESTIONS FOR USING THIS COURSE IN A GROUP SETTING

Select a leader for the course or a leader for the day. It will be the leader's responsibility to keep the discussion moving and to help involve everyone.

Emphasize sharing. Your class will work best if the participants feel comfortable with one another and if all feel that their contributions to the class discussion are important and useful. Take the necessary time at the beginning of the course to get to know one another. You might share names, occupations, hobbies, etc. Share what you expect to gain from this course. Take some time at the beginning of each session to allow participants to share experiences and news items from the week that relate to your study. Be open and accepting.

Don't force anyone to speak. The course will be most helpful if participants willingly share deep feelings, problems, doubts, fears, and joys. That will require building an atmosphere of openness, trust, and caring about one another. Take time to build relationships among participants. That time will not be wasted!

Find ways to keep the session informal. Meet in casual surroundings. Arrange seating so participants can face one another. Ask volunteers to provide refreshments.

Depend on the Holy Spirit. Expect His presence. He will guide you and cause you to grow through the study of His holy Word. He has promised that His Word will not return empty (Isaiah 55:11).

But do not expect the Spirit to do your work for you!

Start early! Prepare well! As time permits, do additional reading about the topic.

Begin and end with Prayer.

Begin and end on time. Punctuality is a courtesy to everyone and can be a factor that will encourage discussion.

Keep the class moving. Ask the leader to move the class along from section to section in the study guide. Limit your discussion to questions of interest to the participants. Be selective. You don't need to cover every question and every Bible verse.

Work to build up one another through your fellowship and study. You have your needs; other group members have theirs. Together you have a lot to gain.

Be sensitive to any participants who may have needs related to the specific topics discussed in this course.

Be a "gatekeeper." That means you may need to shut the gate of conversation on one person while you open it for someone else. Endeavor to involve everyone, especially those who hesitate to speak.

Expect and rejoice in God's presence and blessing as He builds your faith and enriches your life.

INTRODUCTION

Picture two adventuresome girls in full gear, exploring a cold cavern. They mark the way as they follow one passage through twists and narrow rifts of rock. After each turn the temperature lowers. The lanterns begin to provide not only cherished light but appreciated heat. As they round one routine corner they are suddenly confronted with a wall of ice blocking the way. After an hour of chipping away at the glacial chunks, a darkened figure is seen embedded in the ice. A light held at just the right angle reveals a human form. More chipping away and the man's features become apparent through the opaque ice. The lead girl stops in shock, turns to her companion, and announces, "This is the man from the Garden of Eden; this is Adam!" The other girl asks, "How do you know that?" The echoing answer: "He has no belly button!"

The Bible does not really tell us whether Adam and Eve had belly buttons. The point of the story is that they did not need navels. Adam and Eve were not born but were created as adults.

In addressing the topics of science, Christianity, creation, and evolution, we might ask, "Does the earth have a belly button?" In other words, "Does it have the mark(s) of a history it never experienced?" One of the main assumptions of this book is that, yes, the marks exist, but they do not prove the history. "Adam was created with a belly button" is an analogy. When the Lord God created the world by His almighty Word, He created an "adult" earth. Or, restating this truth, the universe was very old when it was very young.

As Christians, we believe that this universe is a creation of the Creator. Therefore, approach your study of God and creation with humble prayer and proper fear. There are times when even Christians need to hear the Word of the Lord which confronts and asks:

> But who are you, O man, to talk back to God? Shall what is formed say to Him who formed it, "Why did You make me like this?" Does not the potter have the right to make out of the same lump of clay some pottery for noble purposes and some for common use? (Romans 9:20–21)

As Christians, we are also privileged to hear:

> For we are God's workmanship, created in Christ Jesus to do good works, which God prepared in advance for us to do (Ephesians 2:10).

1

WHEN EVOLUTION CONFRONTS YOU

EVOLUTION CHALLENGES THE CHRISTIAN

Today, every Christian is confronted with the teachings of evolution—the belief that humans descend from lower forms of life as the result of a process taking untold millions of years. Children in public schools bring home textbooks which openly promote evolution. Physical, life, and social-science courses at secular colleges are taught to students under the assumption that everyone wholeheartedly accepts evolution. Visits to science centers and museums reveal the presumption of evolution. Families driving through the canyon near Tensleep, Wyoming, are almost assaulted by the signs pointing out the ages of various geological formations—ranging from 44 to 600 million years.

The promotion of evolution arises from many places and extends from the subtle to the blatant. Specials on earthquakes, the rain forests, and the great apes actively advance evolution. One television video brazenly begins, "Today biological scientists may quibble over the details of evolution, but they all agree that evolution is a fact."[1] The classic movie *2001: A Space Odyssey* cannot be understood apart from evolution. During its opening scenes a humanish ape slings a killing club into the air. As this bone ascends ever higher, it suddenly becomes a satellite placed in orbit by the ape's descendant.

The assault of evolution may come even from within the religious setting. The following is from the leader's guide for an adult Bible study:

> At this point, if the matter comes up you should point out that the biblical creation accounts can be harmonized with an evolutionary theory of the origin of the human species. It is possible to take the position of theistic evolution, which holds that the Bible tells who created, and the evolutionary explanation attempts to clarify the matter of how things came into being.[2]

Not only is the Christian confronted with evolution in books, over television, within museums, on signs, and at the movies, but also from people. What is to be our "loving" Christian witness to those sons of Adam and daughters of Eve who believe, teach, and confess evolution? What is our response to be when the family is bombarded with the evolution revolution so prevalent in our society?

ATTACK AND RIDICULE OR QUESTION AND DEFEND?

When challenged by the teachings of evolution, we may be tempted to counterattack the teachers. After all, the creation of the world in six days by the Lord God is a personal and dearly held belief, revealed in the Bible, of which the Holy Spirit is the author. In the Apostles' Creed we confess with the church, "I believe in God, the Father Almighty, Maker of heaven and earth"—and we will defend that truth by out-arguing anyone who or anything which denies creation. And if we can't win the argument, then we will ridicule that person so that he or she is humiliated into a position of accepting our arguments. "That'll show him!"

Such a perspective is not an effective witness of our Christian faith and probably does not accomplish much. For example, I am not able to recall the number of times I have "commented" to my TV when a "Nova" program makes a reference to evolution. Yet I changed neither the TV, the station broadcasting the special, the program itself, nor the producers of the program. The only reaction to my verbal attacks were the curious looks from my wife.

The TV, of course, is only a thing. If I were to do the same to people, attacking their personal and dearly held beliefs, their natural reaction would be to become even more resolute in their position. Besides, the winning position of a debate does not determine what is true any more than does the strength of one's beliefs. In fact, the person with whom I am arguing may be better versed in certain facets of evolution than I. In a college classroom setting, the professor has the advantage of using condescension, rank, and even ridicule. In those rare situations in which we might have more information about evolution than our sparring partner, our "defeated" opponent will believe in his heart that evolution really won even though he could not present it adequately. (Actually, this is the same feeling you and I have when we *lose* an argument about evolution.)

Far from rolling over and giving in to those who believe in evolution, the Christian is called to "always be prepared to give an answer to everyone who asks you to give the reason for the hope that you have" (1 Peter 3:15). The reason is Jesus, who died for our sins, not the inadequacy of evolution.

Another part of that word of defense is a witness to the Lord our God as Creator. It is appropriate, as part of our defense of God the Creator, to ask questions. For example, the following questions are worthy of consideration: "Does the discovery of DNA help or hurt the model of evolution? Is carbon dating one of those 'belly button marks?' Which came first: intelligence or life?"

The final goal in our discussions with those who maintain the model of evolution is not to force them into scientific submission. The purpose needs to be the same as for any conversation on the great life-and-death issues of this world, namely, to share your knowledge of the Good News of the Lord our God as our Redeemer. The Word declares that "faith comes from hearing the message, and the message is heard through the word of Christ" (Romans 10:17), because "salvation is found in no one else, for there is no other name under heaven given to men by which we must be saved" (Acts 4:12).

This final goal is extremely important because a belief in evolution (especially human descent from some ancestral ape) could correspond to a disbelief in our creator or a disregard of His vital role in every aspect of our lives. What great need do those people who believe in evolution have? Evolution eliminates the need for God and therefore, any accountability to Him. Such "believers" are in greater need for the Holy Spirit working faith in the heart than learning of some weakness of evolution (like DNA or carbon dating).

Still, in order to share that Word of life in Christ, it may be necessary first to point out the weaknesses in the model of evolution. Pointing out such weaknesses does not create saving faith. It may, however, weaken or remove one of the foundational pillars for unbelief. When this happens, we would hope that the individual would be moved to the point of asking with the Philippian jailor, "What must I do to be saved?" (Acts 16:30). The Word concerning the triune God in general and the person and work of the Son of God in particular may be shared.

A similar need to hear about the work of God in Christ holds true when a Christian son or daughter comes home following a classroom presentation of the "truth" of evolution and the "impossible" claims of any creation myths. The parental task here is witnessing to the truth so that the child, while not necessarily needing to be converted, is confirmed in the faith with solid food from God's Word. That's how parents "train a child in the way he should go, and when he is old he will not turn from it" (Proverbs 22:6).

A WORD OF CAUTION

A word of caution: this study may not be appropriate reading for some young-in-the-faith Christians. Quotes from atheists are included here, and arguments representing the views of secular humanists are presented. Second, it has a PG rating because *parents* need *guidance* when addressing issues like evolution and creation with their children.

This study was written as a starting point for Christians discussing the relationships between such topics as evolution, science, the Bible, creation, and Christian witness. Resources and suggestions for further reading and study are included in the "Suggested Reading List" at the end of this book. Chapter 2 wrestles with the relationship between science and the *worldview* of the Christian. Chapter 3 focuses on the question, "Is believing and teaching creation *unscientific?*" The final chapter addresses our Christian response and witness within the family, at school, at work, and in the community when evolution confronts us.

RESTATEMENT OF MAIN POINTS

1. Every Christian in today's society has been challenged by evolution.
2. Arguing, ridiculing, and finally winning a debate about evolution will not bring anyone to faith in Christ. Only the Good News about Jesus as our Redeemer can do that.
3. The Christian should be knowledgeable enough about the teachings of evolution and the doctrines of Christianity to reaffirm personal faith and strengthen the faith of other Christians, particularly children.
4. As Christians, our goal when interacting with evolutionists should be to defend the Christian faith and to share our knowledge of Jesus Christ.

FOR DISCUSSION

1. What connection may be drawn between society's widely accepted belief in evolution and the corresponding acceptance of antiscriptural positions on issues such as business ethics, human sexuality, and life concerns?

2. Explain the Spirit-driven ultimate goal of God's people as they communicate and build relationships with those who profess confidence in the evolution model.

3. In light of 1 Peter 3:15, what is the best way for someone who believes in the six-day creation to respond when confronted with the evolution assumption?

4. What danger exists for those who claim to believe in both Jesus Christ and in evolution? Apply Revelation 3:11. Colossians 4:5 challenges believers to "be wise in the way [we] act toward outsiders; mak[ing] the most of every opportunity."

5. What opportunities for sharing the Good News have you experienced or heard in situations where evolution is being taught or discussed?

2

SCIENCE AND YOUR WORLDVIEW

INTRODUCTION

Before discussing the relationship between science and our worldview, we need to explain these two terms.

Worldview: By this we mean the basic philosophy a person holds that explains (1) why the world (or universe) is the way it is; (2) the place, purpose, and value of other people in the world; and (3) my own place in the world (or universe).[1]

A worldview based on a god (or gods), on the spiritual, on an ideal, or on the equivalent of belief in a Supreme Being (atheism, Buddhism, and others) is called a religion. Christianity is a religion based on the triune God (the persons of the Father, the Son, and the Holy Spirit—one God, one Lord) as revealed through the Word of God, the Bible. A religion based on the rejection of any god affecting the world (or universe) is called Secular Humanism. It may seem strange to think that Secular Humanism is a religion. However, many belief systems are really religions because they help people relate to their god or spiritual ideal. The atheist religion, for example, although rejecting the existence of any god, deals with God by denying Him.

A person's worldview determines a set of beliefs (doctrines) which radiates out into values, actions, and possessions. Whoever or whatever is at the center of a person's worldview will determine what is true. For the Christian, the Lord God is at the center, and His Word, the Bible, determines what is true. These truths about God, man, sin, Jesus, atonement, and other teachings are beliefs that influence what is valuable and important to the Christian. Confessions of faith are summaries of what is believed and valued (for example, the incarnation and resurrection of the Son of God). Actions follow confessions. Attending divine worship, having family devotions, and evangelism are some examples. This, in turn, explains why a Christian may have a Bible, a certificate of Baptism, a cross necklace, and so forth.

Understanding the worldviews of ourselves and others is important because the outlook determines beliefs, which affect values and morals, which influence actions and determine those material items deemed important. What is it that makes the person tick? Why does he think that way? What does she believe about this or that? With this knowledge we can be more effective in our Christian witness as we prepare the groundwork for building a bridge to the cross of Christ.[2]

Worldview Diagram

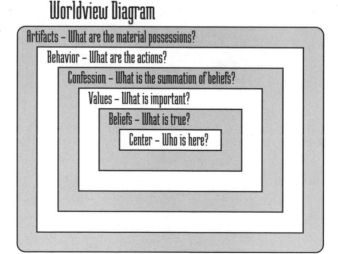

Artifacts – What are the material possessions?
Behavior – What are the actions?
Confession – What is the summation of beliefs?
Values – What is important?
Beliefs – What is true?
Center – Who is here?

Having said that, we need to add that a person's worldview is subject to constant change, even to the point of maintaining two or more at the same time. We Christians, declared by God to be holy, perfect, and saints in Christ, have a worldview in which the Lord is at the center. At the same time, we may have doubts, fears, and sinful thoughts that create a different worldview without God in the center. At such times our prayer might well include the petition which the wise man confessed to Jesus, "I do believe; help me overcome my unbelief" (Mark 9:24).

Science: For our purposes, science simply means the study and subsequent conclusions of how and why the physical world works. The "why" does not refer to the ultimate why, why the universe exists, but rather to a cause-and-effect sequence, such as why my thumb bleeds when I strike it with a hammer.

The scientific method of investigation begins with *observation.* (For example, a scientist may observe that, when a cat is released from a first story window, "something" causes the cat to accelerate until it reaches the ground five feet below.) A *hypothesis* is then formulated about that "something," and experiments are conducted concerning the "how" and the "why." These are tested until a plausible answer is determined—which is stated as a *theory.* (Cats of different colors, ages, and weights are dropped outside first-story windows of various buildings, and the results are the same. "Something" is still causing cats to accelerate to the ground. The "something" is given a name: gravity.) Other scientists then test the theory to determine if it truly does explain the how and why. (They discover that whether a cat, a rock, or an apple is dropped, gravity still works, and acceleration occurs at the same rate. Nor does it matter if the object is dropped from the first floor or the fifth floor—though, to the cat it may matter a great deal!) When the theory holds true for all occasions, a *law* is declared. (The law of gravity, in quite unscientific language, states, "What goes up must come down.")

On another level, some scientific studies are purely hypothetical, even though they are based upon and use universally provable and accepted laws of regular events such as the law of gravity or the second law of thermodynamics. For example, was there a time when Jupiter had a more elliptical orbit; and, if so, what might have been its effect on the earth? Or, to draw on an example closer to the creation-evolution debate, was the rate of continental drift the same 4,000 years ago as it is today? The best that any scientist can do is to construct a hypothetical *model* of what might be the answer. While such a model is based upon the best and most complete use of what is known, the model is still hypothetical. The event can not be reproduced and tested according to the scientific method of investigation.

Evolution, as a study, falls within the category of the purely hypothetical. As such, there is no law of evolution or even a theory of evolution; there is only the model of evolution.

Distinguishing between a hypothesis, a theory, a law, and a model is not merely a matter of semantics. Names and titles represent different things and ideas. Consistently mislabeling something encourages people to ignore or forget what that thing actually is. Business refers to "downsizing," the military to "friendly fire." Whether by design or accidental, calling evolution a "theory" or a "law" implies that it can be verified by the scientific method of investigation. That is simply not true—and to misname it fosters a distortion. Evolution is a model, a verbal description of one way many scientists *think* or *guess* the facts work together. Consistently naming evolution as a model reminds us and our listeners of that truth.

SCIENCE IS NOT THE ENEMY

The Bible declares that the Lord "is before all things, and in Him all things hold together" (Colossians 1:17). The Christian responds by confessing in the Nicene Creed, "I believe in one God, the Father Almighty, maker of heaven and earth and of all things visible and invisible." Among those visible and invisible things that exist, provide order, and hold things together are the Lord's creation of time (Genesis 1:4–5), the seasons (Acts 14:17), the forces of the physical world (Psalm 104), and the order of the stars and planets in the universe (Job 38:31–33). The properties of matter (like atomic structure, mass, boiling points, and density), the relationship between bodies of matter (like chemical reactions and gravitation), and the creation of energy are all parts of His creation.

Obviously, matter and events are interrelated, but in our cause-and-effect world, we humans like to know the how and why. So we observe an event, speculate on its cause and effect, develop a hypothesis, test the hypothesis by performing experiments, announce the results, and perhaps, discover a working principle. Through the centuries, some experiments have given such consistent results that we have come up with scientific principles and laws concerning matter and energy (e.g., fluid mechanics, gravitation, thermodynamics, electromagnetic force).

In a very low-intensity scientific approach, the average person can "discover" the "law" that fish need water to live. More study will reveal that oxygen is needed in the water to sustain the life of the fish—and in-depth research will determine the molecular processes involved in how fish "breathe" water. (The study may help to understand how the curious "walking catfish" can survive so long out of water.)

None of this is either antireligion or anti-Christian. There is nothing ungodly about these equations, principles, and laws which are based upon God's good creation. Just as marijuana, alcohol, and cocaine are, in and of themselves, not evil but a part of God's good creation intended for good purposes, so also matter, energy, and scientific laws are not evil but good. Therefore, science is not the enemy of Christianity in a discussion about creation and evolution.

SCIENCE AND A PERSON'S WORLDVIEW

Everyone has someone or some idea at the center of his or her worldview which ultimately influences what role science (as well as everything else) will have in that person's life. At the center of the Christian's worldview is the Lord God. Radiating from that center in concentric circles are the Christian's beliefs, values, confessions, behavior, and possessions. What the Christian values is based upon who God is and the truths He has communicated (for example, the truth that God created an ordered universe). Confessions of faith are built on these valued truths (e.g., I believe that God has made me and all creatures). Various actions (e.g., praying to the King of creation for a fruitful crop) flow from a person's confession. People have and use whatever is needed to accomplish these activities (e.g., Bible, hymnal, farm implements). Beliefs, values, confession, behavior, and artifacts are all affected by the Lord God being at the center of the Christian's worldview. Consequently, scientific investigation is the behavior of studying God's creation and its design. Although necessary and beneficial, science is not, however, at the center of the Christian's worldview.

Now we are ready to pull back the curtain that covers the center of the atheist's worldview and discover who is there. For some evolutionists, "NoMan" is there in that dark cave. For others, "I" stands at the core. If "NoMan" is there, then the universe has no meaning. This world is a freak moment in an ocean of absurdity. If "I" is there, then "me" is the highest good and "I" is God. But there is no God. Therefore, "I" bear the load.

Far from being an easy burden to bear, the center of the atheist's worldview is a lonely place to be and a hopeless life to live. Listen to the pain as well as the determination to "walk the talk" of atheism in Clamence's confession in the novel *The Fall* (written by an honest atheist named Albert Camus). As you read this quote, ask yourself two questions. First, is science the answer for the issues raised? Second, what do Christians have to say to the Clamences of this world?

> [F]or anyone who is alone, without God and without a master, the weight of days is dreadful. Hence one must choose a master, God being out of style.
>
> I was bursting with a longing to be immortal. I was too much in love with myself not to want the precious object of my love never to disappear. Since, in the waking state and with a little self-knowledge, one can see no reason why immortality should be conferred on a salacious monkey, one has to obtain substitutes for that immortality.[3]

Which worldview is right? As humans, we would like to "prove" (à la science) what is the original cause of the universe—thereby proving which worldview is right. Alas, two problems arise when we try to use science to find or prove this original cause. The first is a philosophical problem. Science is the study of why things are the way they are or why things happen as they do   the study of cause and effect. But, since there is no cause and effect for a first cause, there's nothing to study.

The second problem is a physical one. Science is the process of testing and measuring things and events. To do so, the scientist needs some sort of tool—a device that is something other than the thing or event being measured. But it's impossible to even think of a tool that could measure or test whatever it was (or whoever it was) that existed before matter/energy and caused it to be.

As a result of these two problems, no one can ever prove (à la science) what the original cause of the universe was. And without that proof, we can't prove scientifically which world-view is correct. Each of us has to make a statement of *belief* as to what or who stands at the beginning of creation and, therefore, what the correct worldview is. One's worldview is a matter of faith.

As a related point, the above illustrates why science itself is never the center of a worldview. Science is a behavior, an activity on the outer rings of the worldview diagram. This is best demonstrated by the fact that some scientists are evolutionists and some are creationists. All of this in spite of both using the same laws, principles, and data!

SCIENCE AND INTERPRETATION

To understand why this happens, consider the words of Perry Mason. First, picture the situation. The future of the woman accused of murder was bleak. Not only did she have opportunity and motive, she also had the weapon. Perry Mason stated his problem as defense attorney:

> Once [the prosecuting attorney has] come to the conclusion the defendant is guilty, the only facts he considers significant are those which point to the guilt of the defendant. That's why circumstantial evidence is such a liar. Facts themselves are meaningless. It's only the interpretation we give those facts which counts.[4]

With the scientific laws and principles and all the data being the same for the evolutionist and for the creationist, opposing interpretations are a result of differing worldviews. In the search for the origin of life, unless a person is exceptionally honest and genuinely seeking the truth, the interpretation will be based only upon that circumstantial evidence which reinforces what is already held and believed. Whoever is at the center of a person's worldview determines what is done with the interpretation of scientific data. In the creation-evolution debate, the evolutionist uses the scientific data to explain the how and why of the model of evolution, while the creationist does the same for creation. Although the scientific data does not change, the interpretations and explanations will be different.

Consider the example of the famous peppered moths of Great Britain. Prior to 1845, most of these moths were white with small, black specks. As they rested on the trunks of light-colored trees, the coloring camouflaged them to protect them from being eaten by birds. Only a few peppered moths were black with small, white specks. These darker moths, while resting on light-colored trees, were not as well hidden. The birds easily found and ate them.

After 1845, Manchester gradually changed to an industrial area. Soot and smoke from factories began to darken the trunks of the trees. The dark moths became better protected on the soot-colored tree trunks. By contrast, the white moths became more visible to the birds. Within 50 years the dark moths made up 99 percent of the peppered moth population, and the white moths were down to 1 percent! These are the bare facts.

Note, however, the varied interpretations. The secular humanist reasons something like this: "These peppered moths are a wonderful illustration that evolution is true. Here is an example of the rapid evolution of a species which has undergone a genetic mutation resulting from an environmental change." Evolutionists have gone so far as to print this phenomenon in textbooks and reference books as proof that evolution is so true that it can be observed in the events of the world.[5]

The Christian who holds to creationism comes from a completely different worldview. This individual believes, teaches, and confesses that the Lord God is the maker of heaven and earth. The Christian might reason, "The Lord either created two kinds of peppered moths (the dark ones with white specks and the white ones with dark specks) or He created one kind of peppered moth with enough genetic variation for its descendants to include both dark and light moths. When the tree trunks were light, the white moths were protected and the number of dark moths remained small. As the tree trunks became darker, the white moths were picked off by the birds, the dark moths were protected, and the numbers were reversed. It is a simple, logical scenario that in no way proves evolution." Indeed, the Christian might well conclude that, if the people in Manchester clean up the factory emissions—and other sources of our pollution—then the tree trunks would become lighter again. As a result, the dark moths would begin to decrease while the white moths may, once again, rest easier.

As the example shows, both the evolutionist and the creationist use logic/reason to understand what is happening in nature, but their conclusions differ because of their opposing worldviews.

Perhaps this is a good place to acknowledge that there are people who advocate theistic evolution. They confess a creator God who used evolution as the way life came to be as it is today. The explanation usually given is that the Bible tells us the *who*, while science tells us the *how*. They have assumed a compromising position that, in the end, is neither theological nor scientific. At best, it is transitory.

On the one hand, theistic evolution may be a transitory stop for an atheist on the move from pure atheism to an admission that a god is in control. As an example of this, consider the confession of a Soviet nuclear physicist, Dr. B. P. Dotsenko. When asked if there was anything in his discipline that prompted any theological wonder, he answered,

> Yes. In 1945 I quit the electrotechnical school and went to a university in Lvov to study at the faculty of physics and mathematics there. One of the most fundamental laws of nature that interested me was the law of entropy, concerning the most probable behavior of the particles (molecules, atoms, electrons, etc.) of any physical system. This law, put simply, states that if any system is

given to itself it will decay very quickly, inasmuch as particles composing any system have a tendency to run wild. It means that all the material world should have turned into a cloud of chaotic dust a long, long time ago. I thought about this, and it dawned upon me that the world is being held in existence by a non-material power that is capable of overruling this destructive entropy. I began to realize, moreover, that the most brilliant scientists in the best equipped laboratories still are incapable of copying even the simplest living cell. I started to pray and to worship God.[6]

In contrast to the transitory atheist, the transitory Christian has moved from a position that believes God created the universe by His Word in six, consecutive, 24-hour days (both *who* and *how*) to a confession of faith that denies a part of God's Word (the *how* of creation). This move is spiritually dangerous because it moves away from God's Word and to human reason. Theistic evolution is a perilous doctrine for the Christian to hold. It may soon be followed by denials of the virgin birth, atonement, and physical resurrection of Jesus, since the *how* of such events has no scientific points of reference.

EVOLUTION AND CREATION: CONFLICTING WORLDVIEWS

From what has been stated to this point, it is evident that the confrontation between evolution and creation is not a conflict of science and religion. While some evolutionists may be able to outargue the average nonscientist into thinking that the conflict is between science and religion, we know this is not the case. Many scientists who study the origins of the universe are highly religious individuals, and many of these religious people are Christians. Conversely, some Christians (and believers in other religions) are scientists. Persons in both groups see no conflict between science and religion.

In reality, there is harmony between science and religion. One of the greatest scientists in history acknowledged this truth. Albert Einstein stated that "a legitimate conflict between science and religion cannot exist … Science without religion is lame, religion without science is blind."[7] In fact, science has even led people *to* religion. We read of Dr. Dotsenko's struggle with the inconsistencies between the laws of science and the doctrines of evolution that lead him to a theological conclusion. Honest evolutionists admit that they do not know and they cannot know *via science* whether or not a creator exists or, if so, what qualities the creator may possess.

If the confrontation is not between science and religion, then where is the battle? The conflict is not in science. Science is only an activity, a study of the world (as is the study of geometry). Both the evolutionist and the creationist use science.

To gain a clue as to where to look, ask, "What causes the anger to rise in both the evolutionist and the creationist?" When asked to ponder on the plausibility of a creator as the origin of life, the scientist who is also an evolutionist will typically respond to such an "archaic and far-out idea" with indignant agitation. Such a disturbance occurs because the center of this scientist's worldview has been threatened. (It is the same sort of reaction that the Christian might experience when asked to consider seriously the possibility of evolution. The Lord God, the center of the Christian's worldview, has been attacked.) If asked a question about the "problem" of the ultimate cause of primal matter, the response of the secular humanist is likely to be "Who knows? … Who cares? … Matter is eternal."

What causes the anger to rise in both the evolutionist and the creationist? The answer: "Any ridicule of the person's belief in the existence or nonexistence of God." And that answer brings us back to the diagram on page 18, the diagram on worldviews.

The conflict between evolution and creation is not, in its essence, a confrontation between the teachings of science and the doctrines of creation. Likewise, the decision to reject creation as a credible prospect is a religious one which requires the denial of God as possibly the ultimate and prime mover. (This is true even if those who reject a god prefer to think of that decision as scientific or non-religious.) In the final analysis, atheism is a religion with a worldview that requires the rejection of creationism because of the belief that God does not exist.

To summarize, the true conflict between evolution and creation is the conflict of worldviews.

Two Reasons People Reject Belief in God

Atheists are made, not born. The Scriptures inform us that everyone has the Law written in the heart (Romans 2:15). Each one of us knows that there is a standard that is to be met and that the Standard Maker is a higher power—a god. The conversion of a person from one who fears a deity to the atheist who denies the existence of a god is a rigorous process involving experience, exercising the intellect, and demanding discipline.

One reason some people do so is that the events in this fallen world often seem to contradict a good God who created a good world and who rules over His creation. Christian and Atheist alike have witnessed mass starvation in the Third World, the intense suffering of children in besieged cities, a huge difference between the haves and the have-nots, as well as senseless murders of entire groups of people. We all know individual people who have endured more than their share of pain, sickness, tribulation, and tragedy. There are many people who, like Job, seem to be suffering without cause and beyond their fair share, and we ask, "Why, God?" Even Jesus, in His last minutes on the cross, asked, "My God, My God; why have You forsaken Me?" (Matthew 27:46)

Some people look upon the events in this decaying world and conclude that there can be no god. In Camus' *The Plague,* the doctor and the priest speak after they witness the prolonged suffering, horrifying anguish, and agonizing death of a child:

> "That sort of thing is revolting because it passes our human understanding. But perhaps we should love what we cannot understand." Rieux straightened up slowly. He gazed at Paneloux, summoning to his gaze all the strength and fervor he could muster against his weariness. Then he shook his head. "No, Father. I've a very different idea of love. And until my dying day I shall refuse to love a scheme of things in which children are put to torture."[8]

Experiences like the one just noted either drive a person to God or away from Him. If away, then the intellect must continue and give reason. It may be something like this:

If there is a God, then He cannot be both good and all powerful. If God is good, then He certainly would not permit suffering and evil. But suffering and evil do take place; therefore God must not be powerful enough to overcome evil. If God is all powerful, then He certainly would not permit suffering and evil. But suffering and evil do take place; therefore God must not be good. So, Christian, you must believe in a God who is not entirely good or who is not all-powerful, and of that God I want no part. I choose to believe that there is no god at all.

In the shocking but very real words of the main character in Joseph Heller's novel *Catch 22:*

> "And don't tell me God works in mysterious ways," Yosarian continued, hurtling on over her objection. "There's nothing so mysterious about it. He's not working at all. He's playing. Or else He's forgotten all about us. That's the kind of God you people talk about—a country bumpkin, a clumsy, bungling, brainless, conceited, uncouth hayseed. Good God, how much reverence can you have for a Supreme Being who finds it necessary to include such phenomena as phlegm and tooth decay in His divine system of cre-

ation? What in the world was running through that warped, evil, scatalogical mind of His when He robbed old people of the power to control their bowel movements? Why in the world did He ever create pain?"[9]

A second reason people reject a belief in a god is that people do not want to be held accountable to anyone or anything other than self. This reaction comes straight from the darkened heart that is without Christ, and thus, without peace and comfort. The true religious question about God's existence arises because, by nature, people do not want to be answerable to Him, and they seek to eliminate Him. Therefore, the atheist denies the existence of God. "I do not like the idea of a god; therefore, God does not exist. I believe in 'NoGod.' 'NoGod' is here!" Although some secular humanists accept the concept of a vague god, none accepts any accountability to him/it. As some secular humanists have believed, taught, and confessed:

> Humanism asserts that the nature of the universe depicted by modern science makes unacceptable any supernatural or cosmic guarantees of human values ... Though we consider the religious forms and ideas of our fathers no longer adequate, the quest for the good life is still the central task for mankind. Man is at last becoming aware that he alone is responsible. (Humanist Manifesto I)

> We affirm that moral values derive their source from human experience. Ethics is autonomous and situational, needing no theological or ideological sanction. (Humanist Manifesto II) [10]

When confronted by evolution, whether directly or through your children, the Christian needs to know "where the evolutionist is coming from." The continued denial of God requires a great deal of sustained effort and discipline on the part of the atheist. The goal of the Christian is to give testimony of what has been seen and heard and believed, namely, God our Creator, who holds us accountable, has given us the Good News of forgiveness of sins, eternal life, and salvation—all because of the sacrifice of His Incarnate Son, Jesus.

RESTATEMENT OF MAIN POINTS

1. In a discussion about creation and evolution, science is not the enemy.
2. Science is not capable of answering questions about the First Cause.
3. Science is a part of God's good creation. The properties and relationships of matter, energy, and time are part of God's creation. "For everything God created is good, and nothing is to be rejected if it is received with thanksgiving" (1 Timothy 4:4).
4. Ultimately, science is not and cannot be at the center of a person's worldview.
5. The center of a person's worldview will determine what is done with scientific data.
6. The Lord God is at the center of the Christian's worldview, while nothing, an ideal, or self is usually at the center of the atheist's worldview.
7. The true conflict between evolution and creation is the conflict between worldviews.
8. The true religious question about God's existence arises because, by nature, people do not want to be answerable to Him and, therefore, hate Him.
9. In order to witness to the atheist, the Christian must know what, how, and how much the secular humanist believes.

FOR DISCUSSION

1. What is a Christian's worldview? See Acts 17:24–28 and Galatians 4:4–5.

2. Why is it important for God's people to understand the worldviews of others?(See Paul's words in Colossians 4:2–4.)

3. Why is evolution best identified as a model rather than as a theory or law?

4. Why does the continued denial of God require a great deal of sustaining effort on the part of the atheist (Romans 1:20)?

5. What is the basis of a Christian's testimony? How does it contrast with other worldviews (1 Corinthians 1:18–25)?

3

Scientific, Religious or Both?

Introduction

This chapter demonstrates three realities:

First, creationism is scientific, in spite of the unspoken assumption among both evolutionists and many Christians that it is not. However, the principles and laws which govern matter and energy are part of God's good creation, and the Christian uses the same data that the evolutionist uses to prove a point. Several examples of this will be given in this chapter in order to demonstrate that creationism is more scientific than evolution.

Second, atheism is a religion, in spite of the unspoken supposition that it is not. This chapter will show that the dogma of evolution requires great faith.

Third, evolutionists gloss over gaps in logic and science in an attempt to present evolution as the only acceptable model for the scientific data. Examples involving entropy, time, and probability will demonstrate the lack of logic, reason, and integrity in arguments put forth to support the model of evolution.

Before continuing with discussions about these three topics, a number of definitions will need to be given. The Christian needs to understand at least the basics of what is involved in scientific study (including several basic terms) in order to evaluate how evolutionists and creationists use science.

Regularities: As discussed in chapter 2, certain events are repeatable, dependable, and testable. They are events that are so consistent that people can depend on them. We call them *regularities.* Two simple examples include the law of gravity and the expansion of water when it freezes. Or, as the Lord wrote through Solomon: "Whether a tree falls to the south or to the north, in the place where it falls, there will it lie" (Ecclesiastes 11:3).

Singularities: These are one-time events made up of regularities. Three simple examples include yesterday's rainfall on my backyard, the 1990 earthquake centered in the San Francisco area, and "those eighteen who died when the tower in Siloam fell on them" (Luke 13:4).

Operation science: This is the scientific study of the way regularities interact or operate together. Two simple examples include the pre-space-flight studies on the possible effects of weightlessness as well as the studies undertaken to predict volcanic eruptions.

Origin science: This study suggests how regularities might have played a part in the origin of the universe, the world, animal life, plant life, and human life. Since the origin of the universe is not a repeatable, testable event, the scientist can only propose a model of how it might have occurred. Whether that proposed model includes God depends on the worldview of the scientist.

With these definitions in place, we are ready to consider some of the assertions evolutionists as well as creationists make, doing so under the three topics listed above.

WHICH MODEL IS MORE SCIENTIFIC?

Both evolution and creationism deal with the religious question of God's existence and His role (if any) in the creation of the universe, the earth, and human life. To that extent, neither position is "scientific," because neither is able to repeat and test singularities (for example, the creation of the world, the evolution of a redwood tree, etc.).

However, a person is able to determine, without the Bible and without even mentioning God, which model better accounts for the scientific data and is, therefore, *more* scientific. The question before us is this: *Which is more scientific: the evolution model or the creation model?*

We begin by going back to the quotation by Dr. Dotsenko in chapter 2, which mentions the contradiction between the law of entropy and the earth being millions of years old. The law of entropy states that a system (e.g., this world, the solar system, the universe), if left to itself, will deteriorate. (If you want to see examples of this, look inside some of those plastic containers abandoned for months in the back of your refrigerator!) This fundamental law of science states that things go from a state of order to one of disorder. The disorder of any system is always increasing. This earth, if a billion or two years old, should have turned into chaotic dust millions of years ago.

However, the doctrine of evolution maintains the opposite, that all life (humans, amoebas, sequoia trees, tse-tse flies, camels, rhubarb, bacteria, sturgeons, and the thousands upon thousands of other living beings) has gone from a state of disorder to order, from the simple to the complex. Human beings are said to be the latter-day products of random disorder from an ancient pool. Over millions of years, life supposedly progressed, becoming more complex, more organized, and evolving ever higher and higher. Now, eyes, ears, nose, taste, touch, and brain are so complex that no one can duplicate them in the laboratory. Still, the model of evolution is believed and confessed, even though it is contrary to one of the most important and unchangeable laws of science.

The next question follows quite naturally, *Which is more probable: the model of creation or the model of evolution?*

What are the possibilities that would account for the origin of life? (Take some time to mull over the possibilities.)

Really, all of the scenarios boil down to two basic prospects. Possibility A is that life occurred by spontaneous, self-generation. Possibility B is that some sort of intelligence was first, and that it caused life to begin. In other words, there is a 100 percent probability that either intelligence or life itself is the cause and origin of life.

To determine what the probability is that nonliving matter gave rise to life, all of the conditions for such spontaneous generation would need to be considered. Conditions such as light, temperature, amino acids, DNA coding, time, compounds, oxygen levels, enzymes, atmospheric conditions, water, gravitation, physics, the laws of thermodynamics, electromotive force, chemical reactions, and many other factors would need to be weighed. The results? Here is one conclusion made by two scientists:

> [O]ne must contemplate not just a single shot at obtaining the enzyme, but a very large number of trials such as are supposed to have occurred in an organic soup early in the history of the Earth. The trouble is that there are about two thousand enzymes, and the chance of obtaining them all in a random trial is only one part in $(10^{20})^{2,000} = 10^{40,000}$, an outrageously small probability that could not be faced even if the whole universe consisted of organic soup.[1]

Dr. A. E. Wilder-Smith is an internationally recognized scientist, professor, scholar, and author. He has received awards for his works and takes second place to no one when dealing with the topics of life, information theory, Darwinism, and pharmacology. He is the author of scores of scientific publications, among them *Man's Origin, Man's Destiny* and *The Creation of Life*. I cite his achievements in order to demonstrate that this man is no obscure eccentric. Concerning the topic before us, he writes:

Consider a simple 400-letter gene and let us assume that a monkey is set to pound away at a genetic typewriter in an effort to spell out our coded 400-letter gene, using only blind chance to do so. He has the simple four-letter genetic alphabet at his disposal. The odds against his getting the correct order for the first sequence are four to one. The odds against getting the second sequence right are sixteen to one. The odds against getting the first three sequences right are sixty-four to one. ... For a simple gene of only 300 sequences the "odds against" have been calculated as one followed by 130 zeros, to one. ... It is, then, small wonder that most scientists have come to the conclusion that sequenced DNA and proteins cannot be attributed to chance alone.[2]

What do these large numbers of probability mean? Simply put, there is a 100 percent certainty that some sort of intelligence is responsible for creating life on earth. Because the creation model better accounts for the scientific data, it is more scientific than the evolution model.

WHAT HAVE WE DONE? AND WHAT HAVE WE NOT DONE?

What has been demonstrated to this point in our discussion? First, without any reference to the Lord God, to a god, or to the gods, there is a 100 percent certainty that intelligence of some kind is responsible for the origin of life. Life simply can not generate itself from nonliving matter. The case for the spontaneous generation of life, without there first being some sort of intelligence at work, is absolutely without merit or foundation whatsoever.

Second, the creationism model is the only model that has validity. Someone is out there. And that Someone has the intelligence, desire, and power to create and sustain this creation. And we had better capitalize the name of that Someone, for this Creator exists and is active.

Third, the model of creationism is more scientific than the model of evolution. But, because of their worldview which does not include God the Creator, the evolutionists must ignore the cold, hard facts. The secular humanist likely will respond to this with irritation, anger, or ridicule, because it assaults his personal beliefs that are based upon the center of his worldview, which has no room for a god.

However—and this is most important—even if the above were to convince an evolutionist of the need for a creator, nothing has been presented that could be considered a witness to Christianity. No Gospel witness has been given that would result in a person being brought to faith in Jesus. Rather, the only accomplishment that we might hope to make with examples such as the foregoing is to demolish the foundation for unbelief—unbelief in the Lord God, in a god, or in the gods. A conversion may have taken place from atheism to theism, but not necessarily to Christianity. In other words, we have made just as good a case for Gnosticism (with divine emanations), Mormonism (with human progression to become a god), Hinduism (reincarnation and karma), and New Age ego theology.

If the footings that support the foundation of evolution have been removed, then there is a hole waiting to be filled. A legion of ologies and isms desires to fill the spiritual vacuum. Only when a person asks "What must I do to be saved" does the opportunity exist for the Gospel. This is the time for us to witness to the only gracious God there is: the Lord our God, the Creator who did not abandon this decaying world. This is the redeeming God, who became a part of His creation at the Incarnation. This is the sanctifying God, who re-creates fallen ones by His Word, which brings new life and one day will call forth His own to follow Him to a place and a life where the effects of entropy will be no more.

There is another danger we need to be aware of in our mission efforts. Simply changing what a person owns or altering that person's actions does not constitute effective Christian evangelism either. Again, take a look at the worldview diagram on page 18. If a concerted effort is made to evangelize by addressing only the outer parts of the diagram, then we have not really helped the person, for the center of the worldview has not been changed. Such "mission" work is nothing more than the "white-washing of tombs" and is actually, spiritually harmful.

For example, a missionary may tell a drug addict that Christians do not use illicit drugs and that, if the listener wants God to love him, then he must get rid of certain items and cease doing particular things. (In effect, "Throw that away and stop doing drugs.") The addict gets rid of the drug paraphernalia, modifies his behavior, and thinks, "Now I am a Christian. God loves me because I have quit my addiction. Am I now saved? Certainly; don't you know what I have done to please God." Like the Pharisees of Jesus' day, these people look good on the outside, but inside they remain lost and dead. The Good News of God's love is what the Incarnate Son of God has done for us.

Only when the center of a person's worldview is understood and addressed are we able to prepare the groundwork for building an effective bridge to salvation with the cross of Christ. This is the God who is capable of occupying the center of a person's worldview and changing despair into hope— enmity into peace. Or, as Job has boldly confessed his "know–so hope" rather than a "hope–so hope":

> I know that my Redeemer lives, and that in the end He will stand upon the earth. And after my skin has been destroyed, yet in my flesh I will see God; I myself will see Him with my own eyes—I, and not another. How my heart yearns within me! (Job 19:25–27)

WHICH MODEL REQUIRES MORE FAITH?

The "measuring" of faith is a futile assignment. Our Lord declared that faith the size of a grain of mustard seed could move mountains from one location to another (Matthew 17:20) and could uproot trees and have them hurled into the sea (Luke 17:6). Ascertaining the quantity of faith is not our task here; pointing out the foundation for faith is.

So, what are the bases for the model of creationism and the model of evolution? Answering these two questions will, in an admittedly crude way, give us an opportunity to decide which model requires more faith.

Because faith is the evidence of things not seen (Hebrews 11:1), then the model of creationism really requires no faith. Why? Well, look at the things around you. This earth exists. If I think and therefore I am, then I think that I am here. And I don't have to have faith in this at all; it is a fact. I am on a planet with ordered days and seasons. I look into the heavens and see the handiwork of some great intelligence. Stars and planets make their appointed rounds. By design, moons orbit planets and electrons orbit nuclei. Evidence of a designer is all around me. I have been provided with air to breathe, water to drink, and food to eat. Evidence of a provider greets me everyday. How much faith must I have to believe in the model of creationism?

The proponents of the model of evolution are people of faith. The two excerpts already noted from the *Humanist Manifestos* indicate that there are confessions of faith that religious secular humanists hold. The faith in those beliefs, however, needs to be tremendous because they contradict all of the evidence that stands against them. And, when necessary, evolutionists need to be ready at any time to come up with new revelations. When confronted, the central doctrine of secular humanists ("There is no god to whom one is accountable") must be protected at all costs.

As a result we hear of revolutionary, evolutionary theories such as "genetic jumps" or that organisms (basic life forms) fell to earth in a meteor from some older place. Not only must the humanist be ready to advance changes to the doctrines of evolution, but preparations are mandatory to keep themselves steadfast in their word and work.

Speaking of challenges to a belief system, former atheist C. S. Lewis writes in his autobiography:

> A young man who wishes to remain a sound Atheist cannot be too careful of his reading. There are traps everywhere—"Bibles laid open, millions of surprises ..." God is, if I may say it, very unscrupulous. ... Really, a young Atheist cannot guard his faith too carefully. Dangers lie in wait for him on every side.[3]

While the intellectual exercises of atheists are rigorous, the hardest work is in quieting their human heart. Such a vocation requires the will to resist the ever-present yearning to abandon "human reason" and believe that there is a god. During the disturbing quietness of the night when the doubts begin to creep into the mind—when academic degrees earned impress no one, when subtle points of argument fall into the abyss of darkness—the atheist knows in his heart of hearts that, yes, there is a god.

If such doubts whisper into the atheist's ears during restless nights, then they rise up and roar on the deathbed. This is the time when the atheist's faith in "NoGod" fades and the acknowledgement of God takes place. Sir Francis Newport was tormented on his deathbed and confessed to an infidel companion,

> That there is a God I know, because I continually feel the effects of His wrath ... O that I was to lie upon the fire that never is quenched a thousand years, to purchase the favor of God, and be reunited to Him again! But it is a fruitless wish. ... I have despised my Maker, and denied my Redeemer. I have joined myself to the atheist and profane, and continued this course under many convictions, till my iniquity was ripe for vengeance, and the just judgment of God overtook me when my security was the greatest and the checks of my conscience were the least.[4]

Not only must the atheist prevail over the natural temptations to acknowledge a god, but the battle needs to be fought everywhere else as well. The model of evolution, of necessity, is to be preached at every opportunity. Just as a communist form of government, by a continuous diet of propaganda, dictates what the people think and say, so also the foundations of evolution require a full assault of dogmas through television, radio, textbooks, museums, newspapers, lectures, etc. At the same time, those who hold to creationism must be declared unscientific, religious fanatics.

Actually, these accusations return to rest upon the atheist. The atheist religion is recognized by both the Scriptures and the secular courts. In Acts 17, the apostle Paul brought the message of the Gospel to Athens. Among those he addressed were the atheistic Epicureans. They believed that the world came about by a fortuitous collision of atoms (the origin of the Big Bang Theory?). Paul declared, "Men of Athens! I see that in every way you are very religious" (Acts 17:22). The Supreme Court of the United States has made at least two references to the definition of a religion. While not specifically addressing atheism, the Court held that religion merely requires some belief that is the parallel to belief in a Supreme Being (U.S. *v.* Seeger, 1965). In a similar case (Torcaso *v.* Watkins, 1961), the Court, in declaring its decision, referenced the truth that Secular Humanism, Taoism, and Buddhism are religions in our nation.

What tremendous faith is required of those who hold to the model of evolution! They have faith that their own thoughts determine the truth. They have faith that if there needs to be a new theory to protect them from acknowledging God, then there will be a swell of support from "the congregation of the faithful." They have faith that the unchanging laws of nature do change (e.g., entropy). They have faith that the ever-changing conditions of the world do not result in other changes (e.g., the production of carbon 14). They have faith that they can explain away all the evidence that daily confronts them.

One ardent preacher of evolution (completely aware of the problems with life originating on this earth) stays the course. He and a co-author of an article present us with a confession of their faith in evolution.

> Bacteria and blue-green algae are evolved organisms and must themselves be the beneficiaries of a long evolutionary history. There are no rocks on the earth or on the moon, however, that are more than four billion years old; before that time the surface of both bodies is believed to have melted in the final stages of their accretion. Thus the time available for the origin of life seems to have been short: a few hundred million years at the most. Since life originated on the earth in a span much shorter than the present age of the earth, we have additional evidence that the origin of life has a high probability, at least on planets with an abundant supply of hydrogen-rich gasses, liquid water and sources of energy.[5]

Note the flow of this argument.

- *Declared fact A:* Certain bacteria and algae require very long periods of time to evolve.

- *Declared fact B:* The earth and the moon are not old enough for these organisms to evolve.

- *Determined conclusion:* The time available on earth for the origin of life is too short.

- *Final result:* Since life did originate on earth, evolution has a high probability on a planet like ours.

GENETIC JUMPS OVER GAPS IN LOGIC

The worldview of evolutionists demands that any holes in reasoning and gaps in logic be glossed over. The general opinion of these people is that the earth is somewhere around three to four billion years old. French scientist Pierre Lecomte du Noüy determined that the time needed for one molecule of high dissymmetry to be formed by thermal agitation at 500 trillion shakes per second was 10^{243} years, that is a 1 followed by 243 zeros.[6] (4 billion has only 9 zeros.) Now that it has been demonstrated that the earth is too young, those committed to the model of evolution are looking to the "older" areas of outer space. From the supposition that intelligent life from other solar systems has injected earth with algae, to glacial rockets depositing frozen cargo into earth's ponds of primordial soup, the speculations continue to be out of this world.

Grasping at such straws takes place because the worldview of the secular humanist requires that only evolution accounts for the scientific data about the regularities. But science simply does not know all of the regularities involved. It doesn't even know enough about how regularities interact to explain to me why and how I got a quarter-inch of rain in my backyard and my neighbor got a half-inch. Evolutionary models (and, there are more than one) are only guesses; they are not fact.

Nor are scientists today able to prove that today's regularities operated in the exact same way in the distant past as they do now. As an example, the scientific community was surprised how soon life reappeared in the devastated areas following the eruption of Mount St. Helens. Salmon and steelhead journeyed back upstream according to the purpose given them by their Creator. Plant life reappeared on the lava and mud slopes responding to the voice of the One who said, "Let there be." Elk and deer migrated back within the area. To the delight of many residents and to the surprise of many scientists, the reappearance of life was much quicker than had been assumed. The same type of faulty initial assumptions concerning regularities are used to "prove" the evolutionary model.

An appeal to the regularities of operation science does not automatically lead a scientist to evolution. Indeed, if one were able to approach all the data with neither conditioning from society's agenda nor influenced by the Bible's teaching of a six-day creation, then one would simply, reasonably, and logically choose creation as the origin of life. But our society favors, forces, and enforces the model of evolution. The majority have "exchanged the truth of God for a lie, and worshiped and served created things rather than the Creator" (Romans 1:25).

Not all scientists are convinced that evolution is the true model. They have studied the same data and find ample evidence to support the claim of a sudden creation. There are a number of scientists studying in a field known as creation-science.[7] But, as they honestly and critically examine the various models being supported and analyze the data before them, they realize that they are holding to two differing views. Perhaps the first reaction is the attempt to harmonize them (theistic evolution), to hold that there was an original creation of basic life forms and then evolution took off from there. However, the two views, creationism and evolution, are so opposed to one another that a decision must be made.

In 1977–78 a series of essays was presented on topics ranging from the Big Bang, to environmental fitness of evolution, to the evolutionary tree. As part of his final word in *The Gifford Lectures,* 1963 Nobel Winner and distinguished neurophysiologist Sir John Eccles confessed.

> In these lectures, so far as it was possible, I have followed the materialist story of our origin—nay, of my origin. But I have grave misgivings. As an act of faith, scientific faith, it demands so much. The great French novelist Francois Mauriac whimsically said that it demanded an act of faith greater than for "what we poor Christians believe."[8]

An honest study of life in this world is capable of breaking down the barriers that atheists have constructed. Sheldon Vanauken writes of his conversion:

> Such a relief! What freedom! And atheism was exhilarating: if the gods were dead, then man was the highest. Glorious! And it was a belief totally opposed to that impossible Christianity—a strong, bold creed. But "what" had I said? A belief? A creed? There was the flaw in atheism: one must "believe" in "NoGod." It, too, is a

faith. There is no evidence and, certainly, no revelation; and, by the nature of the case, there can be none. So—I renounced atheism.

From the renunciation of juvenile atheism to agnosticism—not knowing. But with the not knowing, I found—Davy and I found—a truly pagan worship of love and beauty that became, more and more, a theism, a belief that Something underlay the universe. And then at last Christianity.[9]

RESTATEMENT OF MAIN POINTS

1. A *regularity* is a repeatable, testable event that is so consistent people may depend on it (the law of gravity).
2. A *singularity* is a one-time event made up of regularities (the 1989 cutting down of the politician willow tree in my yard).
3. *Operation science* is the scientific study of the way regularities interact (seismological studies).
4. *Origin science* is the study of whether regularities had a part in the origin of the universe, the world, and life.
5. Both creationism and evolution are models, not theories or laws.
6. Both evolution and creationism answer a religious question.
7. Regularities do not account for the origin of life.
8. Whether God is confessed as the Creator depends on the one's worldview.
9. Both evolution and creationism deal with the same scientific data.
10. The model of creationism better accounts for the scientific data than the model of evolution.
11. The model of evolution requires greater faith than the model of creationism.
12. Presenting material which demonstrates the futility of evolution can dismantle the bases for unbelief in a creator who holds people accountable.
13. Destroying the foundations for unbelief is a necessary prelude to witnessing to the truth that the Lord God is the Creator and the Son is the Savior.

FOR DISCUSSION

1. It could be said that creationism is scientific and models of evolution are religions. Explain.

2. "What tremendous faith is required of those who hold to the model of evolution?" Explain.

3. What dilemma exists for those who base their worldview on the model of evolution if they abandon their belief in evolution? Compare with the dilemma of the man described in Acts 16:25–31.

4. What is God's desire as He works in human lives (1 Timothy 2:4)?

5. When by the power of the Holy Spirit unbelievers recognize their true condition, for what is God preparing them (See Acts 2:37–38)?

4

SHARING
THE CHRISTIAN
PERSPECTIVE

INTRODUCTION

This final chapter is written to assist you in not only answering the question "What is the Christian perspective to share," but also the "how." How you respond will depend upon five conditions. First, what is the source of the challenge? Is it from a display or from some individual? Second, who is making the challenge? Obviously, what you say to your grade-school child will have a different emphasis and somewhat different content from what you say to a co-worker during break time. This leads to the third condition. Are you confronted with the task of affirming the Christian truth (as in the case of your child) or challenging the basis for unbelief in God the Creator (as, perhaps, with a college professor)? Fourth, the attitude of the person will indicate whether Law (which demands our accountability to God and shows us that we have not lived up to His demands) or Gospel (that the Son of God has fulfilled the demands of God's Law in our place) should be the content of our witness. Finally, how well equipped are you to bear witness to the hope that is in you— which is, after all, your primary goal?

For Yourself: Know the Word

Be in the Word of the Lord your God. The Bible is not primarily a history book, a biography, a novel, or a how-to-be-a-better-person book. The Bible is a Jesus book authored by the Holy Spirit through the prophets, evangelists, and apostles. From the "In the beginning" of Genesis to the "Amen" of Revelation, its focus is on the Christ of God. The purpose of this special revelation is that "you may believe that Jesus is the Christ, the Son of God, and that by believing you may have life in His name" (John 20:31). You and I have life in His name, and it came to us by the grace of God working through the Word of the Gospel. Therefore we are privileged to confess with Peter, "Lord, to whom shall we go? You have the words of eternal life. We believe and know that You are the Holy One of God" (John 6:68–69). As His disciples, we continue in His Word (John 8:31). There in His Word the Lord God has revealed to us that He is the Creator. Knowledge about Him and His creation is given to us in the Word so that "we will no longer be infants, tossed back and forth by the waves, and blown here and there by every wind of teaching and by the cunning and craftiness of men in their deceitful scheming" (Ephesians 4:14).

Genesis tells us that the creation of the world took place in six days, and Moses affirms this truth in Exodus 20:11. Even "the heavens declare the glory of God; the skies proclaim the work of His hands" (Psalm 19:1). Indeed, the psalms are an affirmation of God's creative work, from the solar system (Psalm 8) to the DNA wonderfully knit to form the unborn child in the womb (Psalm 139:13) to the clean heart created through the forgiveness of sins bestowed graciously by God (Psalm 51). In Job 38–41 the Lord describes His creation of all things visible and invisible—including the Orion constellation, the earth, oceans, weather, and animals (among which is listed a dinosaur or two: the behemoth of the land and the leviathan of the water). Then, Romans 8 tells of the consequences of the fall of Adam on all creation: it has been subjected to frustration, corruption, and decay (i.e., entropy?). Hear the fearful words of the Lord as He puts His questions concerning creation to the man: "Where were you when I laid the earth's foundation? Tell me, if you understand" (Job 38:4).

While the main purpose of the Word of God is to make people "wise for salvation through faith in Christ Jesus" (2 Timothy 3:15), the Word is also "useful for teaching, rebuking, correcting and training in righteousness, so that the man of God may be thoroughly equipped for every good work" (2 Timothy 3:16–17). Therefore, "fight the good fight of the faith. Take hold of the eternal life to which you were called when you made your good confession in the presence of many witnesses" (1 Timothy 6:12).

FOR YOURSELF: KNOW THE WORLD

Christians are people called out of the world by the Word to bear witness to the Word in the world. We need, therefore, to know what the world says, how the world thinks, and how in the world to respond. Being familiar with some of the writings of atheists is important if we are going to be able to present a decent Christian witness to either the secular humanist at work or the son/daughter who comes home from college with some questions after a course in philosophy. If you yourself have not worked through these issues, you will not be in a position to help someone else. In this study, you have already been exposed to the writings and thoughts of some of these writers. The works of Albert Camus and Fyodor Dostoevsky are especially useful in understanding the mind of the atheist. (A suggested reading list with comments is located in the Appendix.)

A word of caution, though: You are going to have to decide what is and what is not helpful, how much to read and when to stop. This will vary with individual Christians. While we are new creations in Christ by grace through faith, our old sinful nature still clings to us. Since we have not arrived in Paradise, we still are capable of falling from the state of grace. The apostle Paul stated this possibility quite well when he wrote, "I do not run like a man running aimlessly; I do not fight like a man beating the air. No, I beat my body and make it my slave so that after I have preached to others, I myself will not be disqualified for the prize" (1 Corinthians 9:26–27). Know your limits, and do not overestimate your strengths. If the reading of one of these worldly books bothers you, put it down. The wise declaration of Solomon is worth noting: "Of making many books there is no end, and much study wearies the body" (Ecclesiastes 12:12).

FOR YOURSELF: WHEN CONFRONTED

When you are confronted with evolution in a public science display that you either visit or view over television, first remember that science is not the enemy. Ask yourself what scientific regularities or true facts are presented that you did not know before. How might these facts be interpreted within the model of creationism? What can you learn about God's creation from the program? Attempt to determine what the assumptions are in the display and where the strongest arguments rest. Are they based upon a statement of fact or upon just a statement?

Consider an example. In the opening chapter of this book a sample of "when evolution confronts you" was presented: "Today biological scientists may quibble over the details of evolution, but they all agree that evolution is a fact." The assertion is made in the opening segment of the National Geographic video *Mysteries of Mankind*. This statement is not fact but propaganda. Even from our limited exposure in this book to the quotations from scientists, we know that not *all* biological scientists agree that evolution is a fact. In addition, the use of the words "may quibble over the details" is intended to give the impression of evolutionists' solidarity, with only trivial matters of disagreement. The impression given is that there are no questions of major importance and that the armor of evolution is invincible. Is that true? Well, you be the judge after reading the following, which is admitted at the end of the same video.

> In the detective story of human evolution we know, in a broad sense, how the plot turned. But we know very little about the chapters along the way. There are too many fossils that are merely fragments; too many gaps in time for which we have no fossils at all. The science of anthropology is little more than a hundred years old, but as it moves forward, it opens new mysteries—poses greater riddles. To begin filling in the numerous blanks, the discovery of new fossils is essential. New technologies will add other pieces to the expanding puzzle. But that is all we can expect, random puzzle pieces. Never can the entire picture be known.[1]

The tone here is much different and clearly casts doubt over the assertion that the model of evolution is the only viable explanation for the origin of life!

A final word is in order before leaving this section. Viewing some of these displays and videos can create some doubts within the mind of the Christian. These works are professional productions and are intended to persuade. Such is the nature and desire of those who promote secular humanism. If you experience such doubts, recognize two truths. First, the model of evolution is not true, even though you may not be able to disprove what is being claimed by the atheist. Second, remember who you are and recall who God is. Reflect on His Word, " 'For My thoughts are not your thoughts, neither are your ways My ways,' declares the LORD. 'As the heavens are higher than the earth, so are My ways higher than your ways and My thoughts than your thoughts' " (Isaiah 55:8–9).

FOR YOUR LITTLE ONE(S)

An old apostle Paul reminded a young Timothy, "From infancy you have known the holy Scriptures, which are able to make you wise for salvation through faith in Christ Jesus" (2 Timothy 3:15). The word translated here as "infancy" really denotes the very young: "an unborn child, a newborn, an infant, or a baby." Timothy had been fed the milk of the Word from the first moment of life. No doubt his mother, Eunice, and Grandma Lois were the spiritually nurturing voices heard by baby Timothy. Let your little one, whether born or unborn, hear you sing the hymn "We Praise Thee, O God, Our Redeemer, Creator." Allow that little one to listen to you reading the Word out loud, "In the beginning, God created the heavens and the earth," and praying, "Create in me a clean heart, O God, and renew a right spirit within me." That little one entrusted to your care, so dependent on you for physical, emotional, and spiritual nurturing, should be allowed to hear the congregation confess, "I believe in God, the Father Almighty, Maker of heaven and earth." The pastor's voice should be a familiar one to you and your little one as he proclaims to the congregation that "Christ loved the church and gave Himself up for her to make her holy, cleansing her by the washing with water through the Word" (Ephesians 5:25–26).

The Lord God Almighty has entrusted this little one to you. He has created life for you and your baby. He has provided for a new creation and a new life by means of the incarnation, perfect life, crucifixion, death, resurrection, and ascension of the Son of God. "The promise is for you and your children" (Acts 2:39).

From the moment of the creation of life until the child steps forth from the house into school, the capacity for learning is immense and amazing. Bring your little one to the Lord, into His church, and allow that one to sing praises to God, because "from the lips of children and infants" (Psalm 8:2) He has ordained praise and strength. Keep your little child in the Word, making preparations for a life lived in this fallen world. Indeed, this is not something that you *have* to do; this is something you *get* to do. What an absolute privilege to introduce your child to Jesus!

FOR YOUR CHILDREN IN PUBLIC SCHOOL

All that has been stated in the preceding section concerning the younger child applies to school-age children too. In addition, these older children need more solid food. The memory work from the Bible, already begun, needs to be supplemented. The spiritual head of the household should include devotional readings as part of family routine. With such a foundation in the Word, both you and your child are prepared for that day when the school teacher announces that evolution is "the truth."

When this happens, recognize first that all children go through the stage of testing the "infallibility" of their parents. Such testing may be the confident announcement that the word *envelope* is not pronounced "en-velope" like Mom and Dad say it, but "on-velope" like Mrs. Phoglea says it. Or, it may be the confused question asked of you concerning the teacher's statement that evolution is fact and creation is myth. Children are exposed to a variety of ideas, beliefs, and values—a helpful and necessary part of mental growth. But they need parental guidance and support as they begin to experience life beyond the home. Give it gently and with respect. You do not want to put your child into a position of being forced to choose between you and the teacher (who, in the child's eyes, is increasingly seen as the repository of more truth than a "mere, simple" parent).

Again, be aware that a normal, growing child asks questions. In response, explain (in terms and ways that your child understands) the difference between fact and faith. The earth exists, and that is a fact. Since no human being is an eyewitness to the events at the beginning of the world, those who believe in evolution are expressing their faith, not facts. Then direct your child back to that part of our faith that is confessed to be true: that God has given us His love in Christ Jesus. As a part of His love for us, He has also told us what He did when He made the world "in the beginning."

A project with your child might help demonstrate the difference between fact and faith. Sit down with your child and draw a picture of a birdhouse. The drawings do not have to be detailed or to scale. Then you and your child build the birdhouse. When you are done, hang it outside. Now you can say, "We have a birdhouse, and that is a fact." Then ask what your child would say if someone came up and said, "Hey, that's a nice birdhouse, but I believe it came about all by itself, that no one designed it and no one made it. That is what I believe, and I have faith in that explanation of how the birdhouse came to be." No doubt your child would say, "No, we drew a picture of the birdhouse, and then we made it. It didn't come about by itself; we made it!" Then make the comparison by asking, "If a simple, little birdhouse required a couple of builders like us to nail some boards together, I believe that this great big world and everyone of us in it has a Creator. I believe that the Lord God is the Creator, don't you?"

As part of the discussion with your child, remind him or her that part of the reason for being in school is to learn what the world has to teach about certain things. Some lessons are very important. While students might not agree with everything (for example, that spelling and grammar is valuable), we still have to know the information taught. So also, while we Christians do not believe in evolution, it helps us to know what other people think.

For Your Older Children
in High School or College

All that has been stated in the previous sections concerning the younger child and those in grade school applies to the children who are in high school and college. In addition, these young adults need even more solid food from the Scriptures and the integrating of doctrine in their confessions of faith. "Solid food is for the mature, who by constant use have trained themselves to distinguish good from evil" (Hebrews 5:14). Other reading materials need to be placed into the hands of these older children. In addition to titles in the reading list found in the Appendix, your local bookstore may have a number of interesting volumes.

Part of the agenda for high school and college students is to train them in independent, critical thinking and to make applications through the exploration of new ideas. Therefore, do not stifle their need to talk about evolution with you. (At their age, consider it a privilege that they will talk with you at all!) Another part of education's agenda is to instill in the students a greater degree of information on a topic than they received in grade school. While this dual agenda works well in the study of certain subjects (like calculus), the results get muddier with other subjects (like psychology), especially when the attempt is made to psychoanalyze you, your family, and the need for religion.

Keep in mind, though, that this process of applying new insights to one's immediate world is normal and, perhaps, even necessary to intellectual growth. In fact, the importance of critical, independent thinking is of momentous importance if the Christian is going to live in this world and resist the temptations to become one with the world. Our young people need to know the difference between arguments based upon wishful thinking and those based on fact.

I highly recommend that you and your older children read and discuss the preface and chapter 1 of Dorothy Sayers' *The Mind of the Maker.* To whet your appetite for these sections, read these three short quotations.

> I have tried to make clear the difference between fact and opinion, and between so-called "laws" based on fact and opinion respectively.
>
> • • •
>
> God has made the world like this and will not alter it, therefore you must not worship your own fantasies, but pay allegiance to the truth.
>
> • • •
>
> It [the damnatory clause of the Athanasian Creed] purports to be a statement of fact. The proper question to be asked about any creed is not, "Is it pleasant?" but, "Is it true?"[2]

In addition to being aware of the agendas of secular high schools and colleges, you also need to keep in mind that, because the teachers and professors are human, they may resort to humiliation, ridicule, and intimidation when a student disagrees with their interpretation or explanation of evolution as the origin of life. When your student comes home having been confronted with evolution, you need to know what occurred in the classroom. Your child's immediate need may not be to defend creationism but to survive ridicule!

In reality, the secular humanist professors at colleges do not want critical, independent thinking to take place on the topic. Rather, they want everyone to agree with their atheist confession of faith. The following illustrates what is commonly taking place.

A recently widowed mother enrolled in a secular college in order to become a registered nurse. Her pastor warned her about professors who deny that there are any absolute truths—and, sure enough, on her very first day, in her very first class, the professor's first words were, "There are no absolute truths; everything is relative." (We might wonder how the professor would respond if a student then asked, "Professor, when you state that 'There are no absolute truths,' are we to take that statement as an absolute truth?")

If the issue raised by your older child actually is creationism versus evolution, you might want to review and rehearse the content of chapters 2 and 3 in this book. Help the student realize, however, that this presentation will neither convince nor convert the teacher/professor. Nor will an increase in one's information about creation science enable a person to win an argument. The typical student will never be able to amass enough information to outargue the teacher. Besides, the professor's belief in evolution is a result of an atheistic worldview, not science. Still, more information will broaden the student's field of knowledge and boost confidence in one's confession of faith. For example, for a discussion of how the earthworm undid Charles Darwin, read chapter 3 in Rev. Gregory L. Jackson's book *Liberalism: Its Cause and Cure*. Darwin discovered that the earthworm was not some lowly creature waiting to evolve into a more distinguished animal. Rather, the earthworm is a highly complex, efficient, productive member of this world.

In conclusion, listen to and discuss any questions about evolution that your older children might bring home from high school or college. Ultimately, you want to help them focus on their relationship with God through Jesus Christ. Him we are to fear, love, and trust above all things.

FOR ADULTS WHO CONFRONT YOU WITH EVOLUTION

It may happen that you are confronted with evolution during a discussion with your peers (such as during a break at work or when visiting with friends or relatives in someone's home). Once again, keep in mind that even if you outargue the person, you still may not have witnessed to them about Jesus Christ. Your main goal is not to win an argument but to share the Word with the person. That may take some time. Certainly it will take a great deal of listening and wisdom on your part.

Encourage the other person to explain what the implications are of their faith in evolution. Some people (but not all) are allured and enamored with the prospect that there is no God holding them accountable. On the other hand, some might simply see evolution as the method God used to create the world (the model of theistic evolution). However, since this model is no more testable than any other, arguing about it will divert you from your primary goal: attesting to the clear word of the Bible.

Having listened to the other person and where that individual is coming from, you are in a position to ask a question (or questions) which will require a self-examination of that person's worldview. But knowing how to ask the question is just as important as knowing what to ask.

Consider the Samaritan woman at the well (John 4:1–30, 39–42). After God convicted her of her sin and worked faith in her heart that Jesus was the Messiah, she went back into town to tell the others. But how could someone with her bad reputation present an effective witness to the Good News that she had seen and heard? She began by saying something that gained their attention and would interest them, "Come, see a man who told me everything I ever did" (v. 29). Then she asked her question: "Could this man be the Christ?"

What God-given wisdom had been bestowed upon this woman! She didn't ask with arrogance and haughtiness, "I—yes, I—have found the Christ; so why didn't you?" She didn't ask with a spirit of ecstasy, "Hey! Wow! I found the Christ! Can I show Him to you?" No, she considered who these men were and what it would take to get them to see Jesus. She humbled herself in the sight of the Lord, counted others better than herself, and asked the question in such a manner that the men might have responded with something like, "A man who told you all that you ever did; He sounds interesting. But, woman, you wouldn't know the Christ if you saw Him. We ourselves better go check out this guy." As a result, many of that town believed in Him (v. 39).

When you understand the other person, where he is coming from and why he believes in the model of evolution, then you are ready to ask your question(s) with a spirit and in a way that interests the person and moves him to some thought. The questions might be worded something like one of the following three (depending of course, upon where the conversation has been going):

1. You know, Nigel, I am glad that you brought up the topic of evolution. I have been doing some reading and have been considering a question about evolution. Maybe you can help me with it. Which do you think is responsible for the origin of life: life itself or some sort of intelligence?
2. Evolution is an interesting subject, Natalie. Should evolution be considered a law, a theory, or a model?
3. Dave, as a Christian I am well aware that I need to take heed lest I fall away from the Lord. Do you think that an atheist has to struggle to keep from believing that there is a god?

After asking the question, don't answer it for the other person. Just as the woman had to let the men go see for themselves, so your friend or relative needs to discover things. Allowing the other person to read, research, and think may take some time. It may also take a great deal of struggling. This is excellent, because wrestling with the issues takes one right to the center of his worldview: "Who is god there: God, I, or no one?" When the struggle starts, then the important questions begin. Of course, be ready to help when asked, but also know what kind of witness is appropriate. Should you speak the Law (which shows us our sin) or the Gospel (which shows us our Savior Jesus)? Your conversations with the person will determine which is appropriate.

For example, one day a man asked Jesus what he had to do to inherit eternal life, how he could earn his own salvation (Mark 10:17–22). Jesus told him to keep the Law of God, the commandments. The man thought that he had done that since his youth. Self-centered and arrogant, he really wanted to know what prevented him from having eternal life because he believed it was due him. Jesus continued with the Law, telling him to sell all that he had and to follow Him. The man went away quite sad because he was rich in material possessions. He was at the center of his own worldview, and there was no room for Jesus, who declares, "You cannot serve both God and Money" (Matthew 6:24).

At first, we might be surprised because Jesus let the man walk away without hearing any Gospel. But the man was not ready for it, and so Jesus allowed him to walk away and struggle with what had been told to him. Jesus followed His own command, "Do not give dogs what is sacred; do not throw your pearls to pigs" (Matthew 7:6).

Consider another example. In the darkness of an inner prison, a jailer asked Paul and Silas the same question that the man in the previous example asked. But the jailer's attitude was much different: he was shaken, contrite, and afraid. He asked, "Sirs, what must I do to be saved?" The two missionaries answered his question with no mention of the Law. Instead, the Philippian man was told the pure Gospel, "Believe in the Lord Jesus, and you will be saved—you and your household" (Acts 16:30–31).

In summary, your goal is not to outargue an evolutionist, but to witness to what God our Creator has accomplished in Christ Jesus. Only when the other person's basic worldview (philosophy, religion, and faith) is changed by the power of the Holy

Spirit—only then will that person be willing to entertain the message of Genesis 1:1, "In the beginning God created the heavens and the earth."

FOR FURTHER DISCUSSION AND WORK

There may be times when you would like to take on some additional work to broaden your perspective on the subjects of evolution, creationism, secular humanism, and atheism. Or, your older children in high school or college might need a topic for a paper. Perhaps you need a topic to discuss with a friend or a relative that might ultimately lead you to present the Good News that Christ Jesus "is the atoning sacrifice for our sins, and not only for ours but also for the sins of the whole world" (1 John 2:2). A few such topics for family discussion and/or term papers are provided.

1. Comparing these two quotations, show areas where the atheist and the Christian agree and disagree.

   > *Atheist:* Moreover, we cannot assert the innocence of anyone, whereas we can state with certainty the guilt of all. ... Believe me, religions are on the wrong track the moment they moralize and fulminate commandments. God is not needed to create guilt or to punish.[3]

   > *Christian:* The first manner of confounding Law and Gospel is the one most easily recognized—and the grossest. ... that Christ is represented as a new Moses, or Lawgiver, and the Gospel turned into a doctrine of meritorious works.[4]

2. Research the following assertion and its implications; then discuss a few conclusions. The assertion: "Entropy began with the fall of Adam and Eve." Does Romans 8:19–22 support the assertion?

3. Discuss the problems of maintaining that viruses, bacteria, flies, Sequoia trees, hummingbirds, tortoises, and human beings

evolved from a single origin. Discuss the difficulties if they evolved from separate origins.

4. Discuss the implications made by an atheist named Romanes who wrote of "the appalling contrast between the hallowed glory of that creed which once was mine and the lonely existence as I now find it."[5]

5. Read one of the following books and construct the worldview of the main character: *Things Fall Apart,* by Chinua Achebe; *The Wizard's Tide,* by Frederick Buechner; or *Surprised by Joy,* by C. S. Lewis (whose worldview changed in childhood, young adulthood, and after his conversion).

6. With the worldview illustration in mind (page 18), consider the words of Jesus: "Woe to you, teachers of the law and Pharisees, you hypocrites! You are like whitewashed tombs, which look beautiful on the outside but on the inside are full of dead men's bones and everything unclean" (Matthew 23:27). What are the implications for our approach to Christian witness and mission work?

7. Discuss what Aldous Huxley, author of *Brave New World,* wrote in another of his works, *Ends and Means:*

> Does the world as a whole possess the value and meaning that we constantly attribute to certain parts of it (such as human beings and their works); and, if so, what is the nature of that value and meaning? This is a question which, a few years ago, I should not even have posed. For, like so many of my contemporaries, I took it for granted that there was no meaning. This was partly due to the fact that I shared the common belief that the scientific picture of an abstraction from reality was a true picture of reality as a whole; partly also to other, non-intellectual reasons. I had motives for not wanting the world to have a meaning; consequently assumed that it had none, and was able without any difficulty to find satisfying reasons for this assumption.[6]

8. As it relates to the creationism-evolution debate, comment on French scientist Pierre Lecomte du Noüy's pronouncement:

> Man does not so much want to understand as to believe he understands. Here again he confuses reason with sentiment, but curiously enough he always prides himself more on his reason, no matter how little he has of it.[7]

9. In the United States Supreme Court case of *Torcaso v Watkins,* 1961, secular humanism is referenced as a religion. What are the

implications and the consequences here for the separation of church and state? ... or, religion and state? Defend or refute the statement, "Evolution should not be taught in our schools, since it is a doctrine of faith put forth by the atheist religion."

10. Evaluate and discuss the "belly button" metaphor used in the introduction of this book.

11. In Fyodor Dostoevksy's *The Brothers Karamazov,* Ivan is an atheist. Consider the implications when he speaks to his brother, who is a Christian,

> And I advise you never to think about it either, Alyosha, especially about God, whether He exists or not. All such questions are utterly inappropriate for a mind created with an idea of only three dimensions. And so I accept God and am glad to, and what's more, I accept His wisdom, His purpose—which is completely beyond our knowledge; I believe in the underlying order and the meaning of life. I believe in the eternal harmony in which they say we shall one day be blended. I believe in the Word to Which the universe is striving, and Which Itself was "with God," and Which Itself is God and so on, and so on, to infinity. There are all sorts of phrases for it. I seem to be on the right path, don't I? Yet would you believe it, in the final result I don't accept this world of God's. Although I know it exists, I don't accept it at all. It's not that I don't accept God, you must understand, it's the world created by Him I don't and cannot accept.[8]

12. Consider taking an independent study course (correspondence course) from a Christian university. For example, college credit courses like cultural anthropology, economics, educational psychology, children's literature, American history, marriage and the family, general psychology, and sociology.

13. G. K. Chesterton admits to being a pagan at 12 and an agnostic at 16. His conversion to Christianity began when he had doubts in the writings of atheists. Compare the following quotation with the one from *The Brothers Karamazov* in number 11 above.

> The essence of all pantheism, evolutionism, and modern cosmic religion is really in this proposition: that Nature is our mother. Unfortunately, if you regard Nature as a mother, you discover that she is a step-mother. The main point of Christianity was this: that Nature is not our mother: Nature is our sister. We can be proud of her beauty, since we have the same father; but she has no authority over us; we have to admire, but not to imitate.[9]

14. Do some reading on the amoeba and consider the way that the amoeba reproduces. Is the amoeba the oldest living creature on earth? Defend or refute the statement: Every amoeba is the original one created in the beginning?
15. Contact one of the following for a catalog of other books and resources available on the topics of creationism and evolution:

Creation Research Society
Van Andel Research Center
Box 376
Chino Valley, AZ 86323
(602) 636-1153

Genesis Institute
7232 Morgan Avenue South
Richfield, MN 55423
(612) 861-5288

CONCLUSION

Does the earth have a belly button? The question, while not seemingly important, does help us focus on what we believe. We could answer, "No, the earth has no belly button," if the question implies the necessity of billions of years for life to evolve in the womb of the universe. We believe that the Lord God created an adult, mature, and fully-operational earth. There was neither a big boom from a collapsing universe nor "a time in the womb." God the Creator said "Let there be," and a complete earth was created instantly out of nothing. So, we could answer, "Yes, the earth has a belly button, because He created a complete, mature universe—an earth ready to be occupied by Adam, Eve, and their children." This is the picture given when the Lord God speaks through His prophet:

> You were in Eden, the garden of God; every precious stone adorned you: ruby, topaz and emerald, chrysolite, onyx and jasper, sapphire, turquoise and beryl. Your settings and mountings were made of gold; on the day you were created they were prepared (Ezekiel 28:13).

During the week when Adam and Eve were created by the Lord God, not only were precious gems sown from His hand, but iron ore and coal were deposited in furrows measured in miles. When God formed man from the dust of the earth, not only were the sources of geothermal energy pocketed in the deep places of the earth, but ocean waves were beginning their first reaching for the shores. At the time when the Lord God breathed the spirit of life into the man's nostrils, not only had He created oxygen for people, but carbon dioxide for plants. When Eve was fashioned from the rib of Adam, the Lord God created human sexuality for future generations. He called huge reservoirs of adult oil into existence by His Word and buried them so they would be discovered thousands of years later. Indeed, this newly created adult earth, this mature earth, was fully functional after six days.

Time itself was only a few days old when the Creator ceased from His activity, beheld His work, and declared that it was very good. Then the Fall took place, and the Creator God would also be the Redeemer God. Years later murder occurred, and the need for this God to be able to raise the dead as promised was graphically evident. Centuries later in the midst of suffering, grief, and pain the confession was made, "I know that my Redeemer lives, and that in the end He will stand upon the earth" (Job 19:25). And "when the time had fully come, God sent His Son, born of a woman, born under law, to redeem" (Galatians 4:4). The Redeemer was placed in a feeding trough and redeemed us on a wooden cross constructed from a tree which God had made. Today, as through the centuries, the church is called out of the world, assembles in worship, confesses her sin, hears His absolution, and sings the praises, thanksgivings, and confessions of Psalm 95 and the Venite:

Oh, come, let us sing unto the Lord: let us make a joyful noise to the Rock of our salvation. Let us come before His presence with thanksgiving: and make a joyful noise unto Him with psalms. For the Lord is a great God: and a great King above all gods. In His hand are the deep places of the earth: the strength of the hills is His also. The sea is His, and He made it: and His hands formed the dry land. Oh, come, let us worship and bow down: let us kneel before the Lord, our Maker. For He is our God: and we are the people of His pasture and the sheep of His hand. Glory be to the Father and to the Son: and to the Holy Ghost; as it was in the beginning, is now, and ever shall be, world without end. Amen.

FOR DISCUSSION

1. In the beginning of this chapter, the author encourages us in our regular and frequent use of God's Word. According to John 20:31 and Romans 1:16 what blessing does God give us through His Word?

2. Why may Christians want to familiarize themselves with the world-view of atheism and secular humanism (Colossians 4:5–6)?

3. When talking with a proponent of a nonbiblical doctrine or teaching, we may be tempted in hopes of winning the argument. Nevertheless, when our goal is for the person with whom we are talking to come to Christ, what must be our first priority (Romans 10:17)?

4. According to God's Word, when do people need to hear only the Law because their hearts are not ready to receive the Gospel? When are people ready to hear the Good News of Jesus?

5. Apply Paul's doxology of Romans 11:33–36 to science to our salvation.

APPENDIX

Suggested Reading List

These books have been selected for this list because they require neither theological, scientific, nor philosophical degrees to understand them. However, they all require study and thought. Second and third readings continue to reveal new insights.

Our reading list begins, of course, with the Holy Bible. Listen to the words of Jesus: "If you hold to My teaching, you are really My disciples. Then you will know the truth, and the truth will set you free" (John 8:31–32).

Achebe, Chinua. *Things Fall Apart.* Portsmouth, NH: Heinemann Educational Books, Inc., 1087. This Nigerian author will take you completely outside of your Western worldview and into one dominated by gods and fears.

Buechner, Frederick. *The Wizard's Tide.* San Francisco: Harper, 1990. Parents should read this book to understand that the worldview of children is much different from that of adults. It points out where and how the comforting message of Jesus is needed by children.

Camus, Albert. *The Fall.* 1956. Translated from the French by Justin O'Brien. New York: Vintage Books, 1991. This recipient of the Nobel Prize for Literature in 1957 gives an honest picture of life from an atheist's point of view. What he has to say in this novel needs to be heard and understood by many in the church.

Dostoevsky, Fyodor. *The Brothers Karamazov.* 1880. Translated by Constance Garnett. In *Dostoevsky*, vol. 52, *Great Books of the Western World*. Chicago: Encyclopedia Britannica, 1952. The author shows that, in this world, both the Christian and the atheist have moments of weak faith. Alyosha, the Christian, wrestles with God, while his brother, Ivan, struggles to remain an atheist.

Jackson, Gregory L. *Liberalism: Its Cause and Cure.* Milwaukee: Northwestern, 1991. This book is recommended for two reasons. First, a section in chapter 3 deals with Charles Darwin's observations of earthworms over a period of four decades and how the earthworms undo the doctrines of evolution. Second, chapter 5 lists logical fallacies that are often used in discussions and debates.

Klotz, John W. *Studies in Creation: A General Introduction to the Creation-Evolution Debate.* St. Louis: Concordia, 1985. Klotz' work is a step up in difficulty from the book you have in hand. Examinations of the scientific and religious implications of creationism and evolution are presented.

Kolb, Robert. *Speaking the Gospel Today.* St. Louis: Concordia, 1984. Revised edition 1995. I include this book on evangelism because of the Creator themes in chapter 1 and because our final goal is to share the Good News that Jesus is the Christ, our Redeemer.

Lecomte du Noüy, Pierre. *The Road to Reason.* Translated and edited by Mary Lecomte du Noüy. New York: Longmans, Green, and Co., 1949. This 1948 French work presents a readable testimony of the impact of science on us.

Lewis, C. S. *Surprised by Joy.* New York: Harcourt Brace Jovanovich, 1955. This autobiography of the author's conversion from atheism to theism to Christianity should be read along with his other, more popular works.

Luther, Martin. *Lectures on Genesis: Chapters 1–5.* Vol. 1 of Luther's Works. St. Louis: Concordia, 1958. This is the best commentary on the first five chapters of the Bible. This readable volume is recommended because Luther believed in a six-day creation, made reference to philosophers, and presents the promise of Genesis 3:15.

Maier, Paul L. *A Skeleton in God's Closet.* Nashville: Thomas Nelson, 1994. Confronted with a discovery which could destroy Christianity, the Christian protagonist uses science, reasoning, and logic to defend the Christian faith in this exciting novel. Many of the arguments for and against atheism are woven into the story.

Romanes, John. *The Life and Letters of George John Romanes.* Fifth edition. New York: Longmans, Green, and Co., 1902. The book may be difficult to find, but it is worth reading. Romanes (scientist and professor) was an acquaintance and disciple of Darwin. Parents should read Rev. Paget's June 15, 1886, letter to Romanes as well as Romanes' reply. Of particular interest are his letters during the last years and months of his life.

Sayers, Dorothy. *The Mind of the Maker.* 1941. San Francisco: Harper, 1987. This mystery writer and theologian addresses the topics of "idea, power, energy, and creation."

NOTES

Chapter 1: When Evolution Confronts You

1. National Geographic video *Mysteries of Mankind* (Washington: National Geographic Society, 1988).

2. James Limburg, *Search Weekly Bible Studies: Unit 3/Genesis 1–17,* Leader's Guide (Minneapolis: Augsburg, 1983), 34.

Chapter 2: Science and Your Worldview

1. View the movie *The Gods Must Be Crazy* for an entertaining example of a different worldview.

2. For an excellent example both of a different worldview and of how not to do mission work, read the novel *Things Fall Apart,* by Chinua Achebe (Portsmouth, NH: Heinemann Educational Books, Inc., 1987).

3. Albert Camus, *The Fall,* 1956, translated from the French by Justin O'Brien (New York: Vintage Books, 1991), 133, 102.

4. Erle Stanley Gardner, *The Case of the Perjured Parrot,* 1939 (New York: Pocket Books, 1947), 112.

5. The account of the peppered moth is presented in *The World Book Encyclopedia,* "Evolution," under the subtitle "Direct Observation of Evolution" (Chicago: World Book, Inc., 1992).

6. Dr. B. P. Dotsenko, "From Communism to Christianity," *Christianity Today* (Jan. 5, 1973), 4–11.

7. As quoted in Abraham Pais, *Subtle is the Lord: The Science and the Life of Albert Einstein* (Oxford: Clarendon Press, 1982), 319.

8. Albert Camus, *The Plague,* 1947, translated from the French by Gilbert Stuart (New York: Vintage Books, 1991), 218.

9. Joseph Heller, *Catch 22,* 1955 (New York: Dell, 1970), 184.

10. *Humanist Manifestos I and II,* ed. by Paul Kurtz (Buffalo: Prometheus Books, 1973), 8, 10, 17.

Chapter 3: Scientific, Religious, or Both?

1. Sir Fred Hoyle and N. C. Wickramasinghe, *Evolution from Space* (New York: Simon and Schuster, 1981), 24.

2. Dr. A. E. Wilder Smith, *The Creation of Life* (Wheaton: Harold Shaw Publishers, 1970), 65–66.

3. C. S. Lewis, *Surprised by Joy* (New York: Harcourt Brace Jovanovich, 1955), 191, 226.

4. S. B. Shaw, *How Men Face Death* (Kansas City: Beacon Hill Press, 1964), 12–13.

5. Carl Sagan and Frank Drake, "The Search for Extraterrestrial Intelligence," *Scientific American* (May 1975), 82.

6. Pierre Lecomte du Noüy, *Human Destiny* (New York: Longmans, Green and Co., 1947), 34.

7. For those interested in a detailed study of creation-science, the reader is directed to the Creation Research Society and Genesis Institute (see page 68 for addresses).

8. Sir John Eccles, *The Human Mystery, The 1977–78 Gifford Lectures at the University of Edinburgh* (Heidelberg: Springer International, 1979), Epilogue.

9. Vanauken, Sheldon, *Under the Mercy* (New York: Nelson, 1985), 35–36.

Chapter 4: Sharing The Christian Perspective

1. *Mysteries of Mankind,* op. cit.

2. Dorothy L. Sayers, *The Mind of the Maker,* 1941 (San Francisco: Harper, 1987), xii, 12, 16.

3. Camus, *The Fall,* 110.

4. C. F. W. Walther, *God's No and God's Yes: The Proper Distinction between Law and Gospel,* 1897, translated by W. H. T. Dau, condensed by Walter C. Pieper (St. Louis: Concordia, 1973), 7.

5. This quotation of Romanes was found under "Atheism," in *Lutheran Cyclopedia,* edited by Erwin L. Leuker (St. Louis: Concordia, 1975), 57.

6. Aldous Huxley, *Ends and Means* (New York: Harper and Brothers, 1937), 312.

7. Pierre Lecomte du Noüy, *The Road to Reason,* trans. by Mary Lecomte du Noüy (New York: Longmans, Green and Co., 1949), 36.

8. Fyodor Dostoevsky, *The Brothers Karamazov,* 1880, trans. by Constance Garnett, Signet Classic (New York: New American Library, 1957), 217.

9. G. K. Chesterton, *Orthodoxy,* 1908 (New York: Doubleday, 1990), 112.

NOTES

NOTES

NOTES

DATE DUE			
DEC 0 8 1998			
AUG 1 0 1999			
NOV 1 8 2000			
NOV 2 2			
AUG 0 5			
NOV 1 1			
MAY 0 4			